Moms Are the Best

Stories to Warm Your Heart

Rebecca Christian * Gail Cohen
June Eaton * Glenda Emigh
Margaret Anne Huffman * Donna Shryer
Nanette Thorsen-Snipes * Elizabeth Toole

PUBLICATIONS INTERNATIONAL, LTD.

Rebecca Christian is a playwright and essayist from Iowa. Her work has been published in over 100 books and magazines, including *Chicken Soup for the Mother's Soul* and *Women's World* magazine. Her new play, "Mothering Heights," is a musical comedy revue concerning the subject of motherhood.

Gail Cohen is a seasoned writer who has contributed to dozens of publications and organizations. Her published work includes articles in *Sunday Digest*, *Family Circle*, and the *Chicago Tribune*, among other titles.

June Eaton is a teacher and freelance writer with a master's degree from Northwestern University. Her published works include contributions to eight books, as well as stories and articles in more than 50 publications, including *Family Digest* and *Parent Care*.

Glenda Emigh is an award-winning freelance writer. For over 20 years, she has been writing for various magazines, including *Ford Times*, *Grit*, *Guideposts*, *Angels on Earth*, and *Response*.

Margaret Anne Huffman is an award-winning journalist and former lifestyle editor of the *Shelby (IN) News*. She has written and contributed to 18 books, including *Simple Wisdom*, *A Moment With God for Mothers*, and *Everyday Prayers for Grandmothers*.

Donna Shryer is a writer whose work focuses on home, family, and fashion. Her articles have appeared in magazines such as *Chicago Bride* and *Chicago Home and Garden*. She is the author of *A Bride's Memories* and *Dad and Me*.

Nanette Thorsen-Snipes has been a freelance writer for 17 years and has published over 250 articles, stories, and devotions in over 30 different publications, including *Woman's Touch*, *Joyful Woman*, and *Southern Lifestyles*.

Elizabeth Toole is a freelance writer in New York City who holds a BSJ from Ohio University. She has written several articles for area newspapers and *Whispers From Heaven* magazine. She is also a member of the Bergen Writer's Guild.

Manufactured in U.S.A.

8 7 6 5 4 3 2 1

ISBN 0-7853-3249-9

All that I am or hope to be, I owe to my angel mother.

—Abraham Lincoln

Contents

7

Home Is Where Your Mother Is

A CHILD WAS ASKED,

"WHERE IS YOUR HOME?"

THE LITTLE FELLOW REPLIED,

"WHERE MOTHER IS."

AH, THAT IS HOME—

"WHERE MOTHER IS."

—*Henry Van Dyke*

The bond between a mother and a child is unlike any other. This bond is so deep, so unshakable, that many people describe their relationship with their mom as the defining force in their lives.

The attachment begins before birth. The child is surrounded by love, carried next to mother's heart. The bonds are physiological and biological yet develop into more than science can explain. Adoptive mothers are no less linked to their children. From the first moment a woman cradles her new baby in her arms, the child has already become a part of her heart.

There are many sorts of mothers. Some bake cookies. Others carpool their children from one activity to another. Still others open their hearts and their homes to foster children or adoptive children. There are mothers-in-law and first-time mothers and mothers who watch their own daughters become mothers. For all their wonderful differences, all moms share a common trait: a heart filled with immeasurable love for their children.

Within the pages of this book, you'll find stories about all types of mothers. Some tales are told from the mother's point of view, some are told by the child. All celebrate the incomparable love between a mother and her child and the fact that each mom is wonderful because she is who she is. The scenarios are different, but the theme remains the same:

Moms are the best.

Nobody Calls Me Mommy Anymore

I realized one day that no little voice called me Mommy anymore, and I missed it. Somehow the word "Mommy" had disappeared from my children's vocabulary, going the way of pull-toys, booster seats, and loose teeth. Even I had stopped saying it. I no longer comforted tiny hearts or healed skinned knees and elbows with a hug and a reassuring, "It's all right, Mommy's here."

Once, when my children were four and eight, I spent nearly a month in the hospital. They met me at the front door when I came home, and they proudly led me to the living room. There, dominating the fireplace, hung a homemade poster that said, "Welcome Home, Mommy." A ticker-tape parade could not have made me feel more wanted.

But today, nobody calls me Mommy; I have become a mom. Moms are different.

They occupy less space in their child's world, unlike a mommy, who pretty much IS her child's whole world.

One day I woke up and my daughter's short jumper swished against her knees as she marched to school, each step proclaiming her independence. Her slender body stiffened with determination, as if to say, "Kindergarten, here I come."

"I can do it myself," she insisted, as she halted me in my attempt to accompany her to the bus stop, "I'm not a baby. I don't need anyone to be with me."

"No," I whispered, watching her march away, "but I do."

Mommies possess all knowledge and all authority. Moms, on the other hand, are quite a bit more fallible. My 13-year-old daughter, in the midst of a mother-preteen daughter squabble, once said to me, "You're my mom. I'm not supposed to agree with you."

"Mommyhood" wasn't something I could preserve in a baby book like a lock of silky hair or a kindergarten diploma. "Mommy" was simply gone, and I mourned her passing. I pressed the word deep inside my soul and left it there like a precious museum piece.

Recently, I spent a week with my daughter and her family shortly after the birth of my grandson. The baby's room doubled as a guest room, containing a crib and a single bed. One night, I heard my grandson stir and cry out in the night. I quickly lifted him from his crib, hoping to soothe and quiet him before he woke my exhausted daughter and the rest of the family. I sat down gently in the rocking chair, which had been handed down from when my children were young, and I rocked and rocked, all the while patting and reassuring.

"It's all right, " I murmured, "Grandma's here."

When I looked up, I saw my daughter leaning against the door frame, silhouetted by the light from the hallway. "Thanks, Mommy," she said.

Heart's Child

Once a year, right about this time, I head for the kitchen to bake two birthday cakes for my daughter, Elizabeth.

One cake is from me. Style and flavor vary from year to year depending upon her preference. Her cake wishes have been recorded in photographs. These pictures chart Elizabeth's growth as well. She began as a tiny pink-and-gold bud of a baby with a white cake to smush with glee, then changed into a toddler who insisted on having a kitty cake—complete with licorice whiskers—for three years in a row. Next came the adolescent who turned her back on tradition and requested vegetarian pizza with candles. And then, in the blink of an eye, Elizabeth became this year's teenager who desired white chocolate mousse with raspberry sauce.

The second cake I bake each year is from Elizabeth's other mother, the one who carried her below her heart and handed her gently over into mine.

The day that happened, as mysteriously as if God had fashioned sunflowers from air, a new person came to live where once there was nothing. A child, this special Elizabeth.

I was forever changed.

13

There has been for these 16 years a wondrous greening of my soul as, no longer a single being, I became a part of someone else, and she a part of me.

And so it's from that miracle that each year I bake these cakes and write an open letter to my daughter's "other mother."

In this annual letter, I update my compatriot in matters of school, activities, growth, and successes, as well as any concerns. I pluck special information gleaned from the journal I keep, sticking in a school photo, a news clipping about a Science Fair award, a swimming achievement. I know that she would be interested, *is* interested, for there's no doubt that the child we share is doubly loved.

Let's just call it "mother's intuition."

We mothers of Elizabeth have never met and likely never will, but I feel I know her. Does she have the same sense about me? I've often wondered. I think so, for when Elizabeth was six months old and had been living with us almost that long, our adoption agency caseworker came to visit.

After hemming and hawing, she pulled an envelope from her briefcase. Finally, after some internal debate, she handed me a set of black-and-white photographs of a sleepy-eyed newborn lying on her mother's hospital bed.

They were illicit photos, our caseworker said, for adoptive babies were not allowed to spend time with their birth mothers in that particular hospital.

"The birth mother wanted you to have these photos," the caseworker explained, handing me a note written in neat, upright penmanship and addressed to "...my baby's family...to fill in the blanks. I love her enough to share her with you." I've always had a soft spot in my heart for the nurse who turned her back long enough for the camera to click.

Looking at the photos, there is no question that my baby came into the world loved and was handed to me with the courage that only another mother can understand: the courage to do what's best for her child.

That's why every year, on Elizabeth's birthday, I've passed along photos of my own.

A mother's heart is big enough to share.

Finders Keepers

I don't remember my parents, and the only home I knew to speak of was a tall red building downtown with green shutters. The only family I had was a row of other little kids lined up in a hallway waiting their turn to take a bath. Depending upon "the season of need," as Miss Ellen used to say, the number of kids varied.

Miss Ellen also used to say I was born under a cabbage leaf out by the kitchen steps so that when she opened the door to gather greens for lunch, there I was. I'd been left by elves, fairies, or the stork, depending upon which tale I listened to that week.

It didn't matter, because I was just visiting. I chose to think of myself as a traveler from the faraway places Miss Ellen read about to us during supper. My parents, I insisted, had left me for a brief stopover en route home. I needed to be ready to leave with them when they came back for me.

Truth be told, the only faraway places I ventured to were several foster homes who found my shy self too frustrating to make a long-term investment in. "She never settles in," explained one lady. "She's like a butterfly poised to fly on." But Miss Ellen had always

cautioned us not to talk to strangers, and these foster parents,
well-meaning as they might be, were strangers.

When I was visiting them I was polite and kept my dress, blouse,
jeans, and socks folded in a tan suitcase someone had left at The
Home many children ago. I carried the book I was writing inside
my undershirt. I think that scritchy sound was one of the things
foster ladies didn't care for. Especially since I wouldn't show it to
them. But, as I told Miss Ellen the last time I came back to her,
I was writing *The Story of My Life* and I needed it close at all times.
I showed her the family portrait I was drawing. A mother, a father,
and usually a brother. Sometimes I changed the color of the
mother's hair and how big I drew the brother and father,
but the one thing I never changed was the small
black dog that sat beside me. In the portrait I wore
my best dress, and my yellow hair was braided
carefully into two straight ropes and tied with red
ribbons. The dog wore a red collar.

I was about eight years old when the
Hendersons took me for a weekend. There was a
mother, a father, and a chubby baby boy who didn't
have any teeth. He smiled at me as I sat beside his
car seat on the way to their house. I got to sleep in a
room all by myself, which they thought I'd like. It was
too quiet, so I made myself a nest on the floor beside the

baby's crib. The next night, Mr. Henderson fixed me a cot in the baby's room. I liked hearing his snores. I drew "ZZZs" above the baby's head in my family portrait. I worked on it a lot that weekend and the next time I came to visit, too. The mother was getting to look a lot like Mrs. Henderson, who said I could call her Mollie. Mr. Henderson was Tom. The baby they called Jake.

Adoption, Miss Ellen said, is when a family decides to keep you. The Hendersons wanted to adopt me. I didn't tell Miss Ellen good-bye because I knew I would be back. I always was.

I was polite to the judge who asked how I liked living with the Hendersons. "Fine," I said, "but I'm just visiting." And it was fine. I slept in baby Jake's room but kept my things in what the Hendersons called my room. It was lilac and pink, my favorite colors. I colored the background of my family portrait to match. I put my crayons in the top drawer of the empty dresser but kept my suitcase under my cot in Jake's room; *The Story of My Life* was getting so thick I asked Mrs. Henderson for a paper sack to carry it in. She made me a draw-string bag. Turquoise, another of my favorite colors.

One day, after I came in from the backyard where I had been pushing baby Jake in his swing, there was a box on the floor of my room. It was tied with a pretty bow. Mrs. Henderson stood in the doorway. "Open it," she said, smiling.

I carefully unwrapped it, folding the wrapping paper neatly so I could use it to make a cover for *The Story of My Life.* Inside the box was a big ball of string. That was all. A piece of string led through a hole in the bottom of the box.

"Why don't you see where it takes you," invited Mrs. Henderson, scooping up baby Jake.

Holding the string like a fishing line, I followed it all the way to the den, where it was wrapped around lamps, chairs, and the television, out to the kitchen, back upstairs, and finally out the back door to the garage.

There, with the string tied to its red collar, was a curly black dog.

"Mine?" I asked, scarcely daring to breathe.

"To keep. Like you," my new mother said. "Forever."

19

A MOTHER UNDERSTANDS WHAT A CHILD DOES NOT SAY.

—*Jewish proverb*

The Birth of a Mother

I t was a long delivery. Gina could no longer recall the moments before, nor could she imagine the moments after. It was her first child's birth day. Despite her desire to see her baby—and, most of all, to end this labor—this infant had clearly decided to "live in."

Before the doctor got serious, sending family members out of the cozy, country-decorated birthing room, Gina's only breaks came as quick, panicked glances toward her husband, Don, and toward her mother, who had arrived five hours before, ready to hold her hand, caress her brow, and feed her ice chips. Gina liked the fact that her mom was near. Moms have a power, she thought. Any time now, Gina reminded herself, she herself would possess such powers.

Labor had been going on for hours. After near exhaustion—both infant and mother—the doctor ordered an emergency cesarean delivery. Only fathers were allowed in the operating room, the doctor said. Gina's mom would have to wait in the waiting room. As Gina was wheeled into the operating room, she clutched at her mom in a panic, but the doors swung shut behind her.

Ten minutes later, a perfect baby girl came into the world. As soon as Don saw that everyone was okay, he ran into the hall to tell everyone the news. Upon inspecting the healthy infant, however,

a nurse drew in her breath and said, "Ohhh my! We have a cone head." Gina's world crashed. A cone head! She would find specialists, the best in the world. She watched as her baby girl was carried off by a team of serious nurses and doctors.

That's when Gina's mother bustled back into the room, full of pride and ready to see her granddaughter. In tears, Gina fell into her mother's arms and wept. Her child had a cone head!

Wiping her daughter's tears, Gina's mother fought back the urge to smile. There would be plenty of time tomorrow to tease Gina gently about her confusion. For now, though, she simply explained that this cone shape would be gone within the hour—it was a common occurrence and nothing to worry about.

Once Gina was sleeping soundly, her mother allowed her smiles to come out. She had her first granddaughter, someone to spoil silly. She had a grown daughter who was ready to defend a little girl's life. The smiles became giggles, and the giggles became laughter. This, Gina's mother thought, was going to be a long, long delivery into motherhood.

The Scent of Yesterday

I remember my first real date so clearly. Well actually, the date itself is a wee bit sketchy in my mind, and exactly what we did and where we went is even hazier, but I do remember getting ready for the date. It was the spring of 1970, and the details remain as vivid as a freshly picked bouquet.

I remember taking a shower and meticulously blowing dry each individual hair. I remember wearing a white shirt tucked into bright red-and-white polka dot hip-hugger bell bottoms. I remember standing in front of the mirror, wondering what the evening would bring, when my mother walked into the room. As she perched on the side of my bed, I fully expected the mother of all talks. But she knew, as I did, that the talks had been talked and the lectures supplied. I was 15, and I knew all about the birds and the bees, the do's and don'ts, the can's and cannot's. It was show time, and if memory serves me, I think I recall Mom enjoying just a little motherly pride. Her oldest daughter was preparing for her first date. The training wheels had been removed.

So, instead of delivering a speech, Mom simply commented on how pretty I looked and then offered her bottle of perfume. The one bottle on her vanity my sister and I were not allowed to play with. As she gently dabbed my pulse points, the sweet smell of lilies of

the valley filled the room. It was the same scent I'd smelled for years, whenever Mom entered a room. It was the scent of arms around me—when I cried, when I could not grasp algebra, when nasty kids were mean to me. It was the first fragrance I sensed when Mom snapped my bedroom shades each morning and the last scent I experienced before the lights went out each night. It was a perfume that, oddly enough, came with my own first home, since the previous owners had surrounded the entire east side of the yard with a carpet of lilies of the valley.

The date? It went well enough. Nothing too monumental, but pleasant if memory serves. What I do remember, though, is the smell of lilies of the valley. I was on my own yet not alone, for every time my wrist moved near my face I inhaled the trust and confidence and sheer pleasure my mother showed in letting me grow up.

WHEN GOD THOUGHT OF MOTHER,
HE MUST HAVE LAUGHED WITH SATISFACTION...
SO RICH, SO DEEP, SO DIVINE,
SO FULL OF SOUL, POWER, AND BEAUTY,
WAS THE CONCEPTION.

—*Henry Ward Beecher*

23

Self Portrait

Shaking her head, Jessica can't imagine what she had been thinking. "If you don't intend for a child to play with a toy, why give it to him in the first place?" she'd asked herself again and again. She admits she didn't know what she'd thought Charlie, a five-year-old, joyous, budding artist, would do with the new easel and paints she had so painstakenly chosen for him as a surprise "big boy" birthday gift. He'd been so thrilled, the look of joy on his face all that she'd hoped for and more. But when she saw him open up the paint before she had a chance to put newspaper down to protect the carpet, when she saw him happily painting away in his brand new clothes—the smock she had so thoughtfully provided still folded neatly beside him—when she saw the paint-spattered carpet, the paint-spattered walls, the paint-spattered clothes . . . she'd lost it.

She winced in memory of her outburst, for Charlie had only been enjoying his gift. From her. Ever since she had berated him for the mess he had made and made him stop painting right then and there so she could start cleaning up—well, ever since then Charlie had

refused to even look at his easel or touch his paints. It had gotten so bad that his crayons sat unused in a box in the corner of the playroom, forlorn and abandoned.

Weeks passed. Charlie refused to use the easel, no matter how Jessica coaxed. And when he finally did go near the lovely wood structure, it was to use it as a goalpost for a makeshift soccer game.

Jessica looked at her refrigerator, decorated from top to bottom with artwork Charlie had created over the past few years, and finally had an idea of how she might interest him in art again.

When Charlie got home from school, Jessica greeted him at the door.

"I've got a surprise for you," she said, ushering him into his bedroom.

She supressed a smile as she watched Charlie's eyes widen, taking in the sight before him. The wallpaper had been stripped from the walls, and open cans of paint sat everywhere, with wide-bristled paintbrushes set invitingly beside them. A huge plastic sheet covered the floor.

25

"Come on," Jessica invited casually. "Let's have some fun."

Charlie eyed her suspiciously. "No," he said stubbornly. "It's too messy."

"Oh, come on," his mom coaxed. "I'll go first. Watch me!" With that, Jessica dipped a paintbrush into the brightest color she could find and began stroking reckless shapes on the nearest wall.

Charlie giggled.

She dropped her brush, grabbed a second one, and began adding huge blue dots to her design, disregarding the paint dripping on her shoes and on the floor. By the third or fourth color, she noticed that Charlie had dropped his bookbag and joined in the fun.

Jessica quietly set down her paintbrush and grinned in delight as she watched Charlie fling paint on the walls, whooping in glee.

Whether his budding artistic talent will eventually bloom into something more remains to be seen, Jessica thought with satisfaction, but whatever he uses this artistic flair for—if he grows up to be a famous artist, or a housepainter, or even just someone who likes to doodle on a notepad as he talks on the phone—who am I to stifle his creativity?

Can You Hear What I Hear?

Different" is not a good thing to be when you are a child.

Just ask Jocelyn, a small, dark-haired child whose family had just moved into the old Fleming place on the corner.

We mothers, talking on the party-line or out on our porches, felt sorry for Jocelyn. She lived in a silent world that she watched with large, dark eyes. A world that didn't include the sounds everyone else took so much for granted.

For weeks after she and her family moved in, we could see the child looking out the bay window onto the street or sitting on the porch stoop gazing at the clouds above her head. Sometimes we'd see her walking past our houses, holding on to her mother's hand, on the way to Mackenzie's grocery store. The mother was friendly enough, but the child just put her head down and kept walking.

The person we felt the most sorry for was Jocelyn's mother, Lois. That poor woman, even though she kept her head held high and a smile on her face all the time, was suffering on her little girl's behalf. You could read it in her eyes, in the quick look of pain when she saw our children running all over everywhere like a bucket of ants, calling to one another and laughing and playing in the summer sun.

We tried to get our children to play with Jocelyn, but they quickly grew bored when she didn't catch on or fell behind. It was either include her, I finally told my Ronnie and Karen, "or else." One day, they forgot she couldn't hear them telling her they were leaving and left her alone on the playground.

I had to admit, and the other mothers agreed, how could the children ever understand one another? Sad as it might be, the gap was too wide.

I reckoned without Jocelyn's mother.

Using hands that danced like doves on the air, Lois built a bridge to span that gap. As I told the ladies over coffee the other morning, I'll go ahead and be the first to admit I was wrong to doubt it could happen.

Lois started bridging the gap with an invitation to all the neighborhood children to come to a party.

Kids being what they are, they all went. When my Ronnie and Karen came home, they were bursting with talk. Actually, their talking was more like birds flapping their wings. They were "talking" with their hands. It seemed, when I finally got them to speak in a language I could understand, that Jocelyn and her mother spoke in a special code. A code, my excited children said, they were going to learn, too.

Well, I got on the party-line right away. Sure enough, all the other kids were excited to learn this code.

And so the summer went. Our rowdy kids sitting eagerly at the picnic table over in Jocelyn's backyard learning sign language. The rest of us leaned over our fences and watched, often unable to keep our own hands still. In time, we picked up more than a little of this special code. My, oh my, what a smile lit up Jocelyn's face when I raised my hand in that universal symbol, "I love you."

It was a special joy and quite a coup for the neighborhood that fall when our children "sang" a song in this new language at the talent show at the county fair. Jocelyn was the proudest of them all when she was tapped on the shoulder and told that her group had just won first prize. Or was Lois the proudest? It wasn't that hard to look behind the secretive smile on her face, as she watched Jocelyn and the other children hugging and cheering, and understand what she was feeling.

The Ghost of Christmas Past

A few weeks before Christmas one year, my husband and I visited a quaint town in the north Georgia mountains. At a country Christmas store, I found exactly what I wanted—a large artificial tree adorned with mauve ornaments, ribbons, and lace. The tree towered over all the others and was—in a word—majestic.

Staring up at it, I knew I must have that tree. I deserved it! After all those years of plain-Jane Christmas trees, I would have the best. This glorious designer tree would look spectacular in its place of honor in front of the bay window. Surely my grown children would be glad to leave all those old handmade ornaments in the basement. I certainly wouldn't miss dragging out that 15-year-old construction paper chain or the clothespin reindeer with its missing eyes. Gone would be the tinfoil bell and my son's metal star.

Picturing these ornaments, I smiled. Though it's been years now, I can still see Nathan's dad holding a nail while Nathan patiently hammered his name across a cut-out star. "Mama, look!" he shouted when he finished. His eyes shone bright as he handed me his treasure.

And that clothespin reindeer! My daughter had almost exploded with joy as she explained, step by step, how she created the little reindeer for me at school. Another time, she had made a Christmas bell ornament from a miniature flowerpot she had decorated with green and red rickrack.

One year, both of my kids and I sat for hours cutting Christmas stockings out of felt. Those stockings, featuring my children's names boldly—if a little sloppily—in glitter, were somewhere in that box of time-worn and faded ornaments.

I recalled a plaster mold of Nathan's hands—with his name and age (five) scrawled on the back—that I always hung in a place of honor on the front of the tree.

I looked again at the stately tree adorned in mauve ornaments and lace. Suddenly, it began to lose its luster. It looked very nice there in that store, but that's where it would stay.

Christmas brought my adult children home that year. Laughter filled the family room as we decorated the sweet-smelling cedar Christmas tree we had chopped down just that afternoon—the whole family together. "Look, Mom," my daughter said, beaming at me. She giggled as she hung the plaster mold in its usual place of honor.

I looked at our tree with satisfaction, knowing that no more beautiful Christmas tree had ever existed.

ABCs

e talked it over and decided that if our mother, Amelia Grey, wanted to go to school, it was okay with us.

I was ten years old at the time (that's me, Ethan), and my twin sisters, Nikki and Nina, were seven. We lived above a card shop in a small apartment in the middle of town.

The night before her first day of classes, Mama was nervous. She talked about feeling tingly in her stomach, just below her ribcage. The twins and I smiled knowingly. We knew how that could be!

Mama was worried about school, mainly because she was older than most of the other college students. She told us she thought she would be an outsider, "a piccolo in the tuba section," she called it.

When we asked her why she was going back to school anyway, she told us she wanted to give us a better life. She wanted to become a teacher, so that she could give lots of children a chance at a better life. For that, she explained, she needed a college degree. Right now Mama was a cashier in a restaurant and sold beauty products on the side. I could tell it was hard work; by the end of the day she was sometimes so tired she would collapse in her favorite chair after making dinner—too tired to do anything more than watch us kids

play. Even with Mama's second job, we were often a little short of money by the end of the month.

So when it was time for Mama to leave for her first day of school, we lined up in the hallway by the front door to see her off. After she hugged and kissed us goodbye, we gave her a present: a bookbag we had spruced up by taping the frayed parts together with neon tape and decorating it with stickers. As Mama walked down the sidewalk, bookbag slung proudly over her shoulder, we waved good-bye through the window and flashed her the thumbs-up sign.

When Mama returned home later that day, she had a present for us! She had bought four T-shirts displaying her college logo—one for each member of the family. We all wore them that night as we ate supper, celebrating Mama's first day of school.

* * *

One Tuesday night (the night I always went to campus with Mama), I was trying to finish my homework when I came across a word I didn't recognize. As I tried to puzzle out the meaning of the word, I must have looked really confused, because a professor stopped by the chair where I always sat and asked if I needed any help.

He'd seen me before, he said, a little question mark at the end of his words like a fishing hook. So I told him about Mama going to school and how when I came with I always sat where she could see me. Sure enough, she was looking right now. The professor and I both waved. I told him how the twins only got to come once in a while because they needed to go to bed earlier but sometimes they slept here on a couch. On the nights when class ran really late, we'd all fall asleep on the bus on the way home—Mama included.

Mama didn't like to bring us to her night classes, but she always said at least then she knew where we were. We spent the time doing our homework, reading books, and talking a lot about how smart Mama was and how great life would be when she became a teacher.

* * *

34

When Mama finally graduated, we were all so proud of her our faces hurt from grinning. We wanted to sit in the front row, where she could see us when she walked across the stage to get her diploma, but Mama said no. We couldn't believe it! All those years of going to college with Mama—doing our homework on the floor outside her classroom, sleeping on the uncomfortable benches on the bus—and Mama wasn't going to let us watch her graduate?

No, she told us, you can't sit in the front row, and I'll tell you why. You belong up on the stage with me, that's why. I couldn't have

earned this diploma without your help and your support, so it belongs to you as much as it belongs to me.

It belongs to all of us, she continued, as she wrapped her arms around me and the twins and squeezed really tight, because we all had learned from this college experience.

As we walked across the sun-dappled stage to accept our diploma, I knew that Mama was the smartest woman in the whole world.

A MOTHER IS NOT TO BE COMPARED WITH ANOTHER PERSON—SHE IS INCOMPARABLE.

—*African proverb*

35

The Power of Love

We might as well live in a tree.

Fear of owls has sent our youngest daughter, Julia, into a frenzy. Adrienne, my wife, has decided to educate not only the child but our whole family about these night-roaming creatures. In the process, we've spent a lot of time peering at the maple and oak trees in our yard.

Spring is family-raising time for all critters, even the usually shy owls. We hear them call one another along the river on whose banks we live, but we seldom see them. One small brown-and-white owl, however, put in a personal appearance as a monster—at least according to Julia—with claw feet, razor-sharp beak, and a voice to chill the blood as it shrieked, "Whooooooo?"

In this case, whoooo it terrified was Julia, who was playing outdoors about dusk. Unknowingly, she passed too close to the owl's nest. The owl's warning sent the child screaming into the house.

If that wasn't enough, the mother owl launched a swooping attack several days later. From then on, Julia refused to set foot outside unaccompanied.

That's when Adrienne suggested, "Let's hit the books."

Videos, books, the zoo. We did it all, even gently touching an injured owl at the Children's Museum as it perched on the handler's glove. Through our exhaustive study, we learned a lot about owls.

And about one another.

What no one but me knows is that Julia's fear is pale compared to her mother's. Adrienne has been terrified of birds ever since she was attacked by geese as a child. If a creature has feathers, Adrienne fears it. But apparently not in front of her child.

And so when I watch Adrienne and Julia read to each other, watch videos, or fill in between the lines of a nature coloring book, I know that Adrienne is taming her own fears as well. In doing so, I've learned from her, this brave woman I married, that to name a fear is to know it, and to know it is to beat it. Which is how Julia has been led from nighttime terrors into daylight curiosity and explanations.

One thing, however, defies explanation: the power of love that a mother has for her child—a love that led Adrienne and Julia to be sitting tonight on the back porch trying to call the owls closer.

How, I asked myself when I realized what they were doing, can anyone explain the power of that kind of love?

It's as natural as an owl in a tree, according to Adrienne: A mother does all she can to protect her nestling.

37

"What I Learned About My Mother"

by Phoebe Erin McNichols, Grade 7

My grandma says I won't really know my parents until I'm as old as they are, but I don't know how that can be true. After all, I've lived with them for 12 whole years. I know that my dad snores really loud and that my mom reads romance novels while she takes a bubble bath. I bet grandma doesn't know either of those things. And she doesn't know about this either: When I go back to school, if I have to write a report on what I did on my summer vacation, I will call it "What I Learned About My Mother." And it will be very interesting.

My mother has an associate's degree and someday wants to be a nurse. (It's a good thing that she doesn't want to be a teacher because she doesn't spell very well.) She really likes helping people, and she wants to work in a

cardiac care unit. Her dad had a heart attack when she was very young, so that's probably why. She has one brother and one sister, and all three of them grew up on a farm. Her hobbies are gardening and sewing, and when she was little she had polio. She has perfectly straight teeth—and never once had a cavity. Her grandparents are from Ireland, and they came to the United States just after they got married.

My mother didn't marry my father because she didn't love him.

But she really, really loves me, and that's why she let my parents adopt me, and that's why she wrote me a letter on the day I was born.

I always knew I was adopted, and that made me very special. But I didn't know anything about my birth mother until I read her letter. It had been stored away with the other adoption papers from the court, and our social worker said I could read it "when I was old enough to understand."

My mom and dad adopted me when I was only four days old (they couldn't bring me home from the hospital for a week after that, though, because I had jaundice and was as yellow as a banana). Once they got me home, all of my aunts and uncles and

grandparents and cousins had a big party for me. Everyone wanted to hold me, and my Uncle Kyle even counted all of my fingers and toes. I saw that on the video my dad and grandpap made of my adoption party. I love to watch that video—it was the first one I ever saw. There were lots of pink and white balloons and everyone was having fun, even though I was mostly just sleeping. There was a cake with white icing and a pink rose next to my name, which was written in cursive. The cake was bigger than I was—everyone said that to the camera. Penny, my stuffed bear from when I was little, sat on my green rocking chair with balloons tied to her paw.

It was right after my 12th birthday party that my parents gave me my mother's letter. Everyone kissed me goodbye, and Dad put away the video camera while Mom cleared the table. Then we sat out on the front porch like we always do. That's when they told me about it. Dad asked me if I thought I wanted to read it, and my mom said she thought I was ready because I'm mature for my age. They said that since it's summer and school is out, I'd have time to think about her and talk to them about her before I go back to school in September. And then they were quiet. Dad put his arm around my shoulder and pulled me close to him. I could see an envelope in the pocket of his denim shirt.

And so I read the letter. It was written in violet ink on plain white stationery, and the date in the corner was my birth date. She signed it, "I will love you always." The three of us sat on the steps together,

looking at the piece of white paper on my lap. We read it again, then Dad asked if I'd like to keep it in my room or put it in the wooden box with my birth certificate, our adoption papers, and their insurance policies. I thought the wooden box would be best.

I do think about her—my other mother. Especially at night, when I brush my perfectly straight teeth. And just before I go to sleep, when I say my prayers. I am thankful that she chose my mom and dad. And I hope that wherever she is, she's just as happy as I am that she let them adopt me.

❦

THE HAND THAT ROCKS THE CRADLE IS THE HAND
THAT RULES THE WORLD.

—*William Ross Wallace*

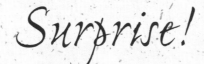

I found my old diary the other day. The burgundy, imitation leather one. The key had disappeared years ago, so I used a paper clip to break into my long-ago secrets.

I got the diary for my 11th birthday—the last birthday I celebrated in the house where I was born, and where my brothers and sister and I had spent most of our childhood.

"Dear Diary," I'd written, "the past looks better than the future."

It sounds a bit grown-up, so I suspect it was a phrase I'd overheard from one of the adults who were ruining my life that summer by breaking up our family. We kids were to go with our mother, while our father was set to remarry three weeks after the divorce. The future looked grim, no matter how you put it.

Worst of all for me was having to leave my best friend, Amy Sue. We were born the same

month, and our mothers were best friends. We had grown up together and considered each other soulmates. We "belonged" to one another's families.

I thought leaving her was the worst until we moved from our spacious old house into a stuffy, third-floor apartment that had no eastern windows. For the first time in my life, I awoke without ever seeing the dawn out my window. If that weren't bad enough, I started a new school. It was all made bearable, as my diary knew so well, because Amy Sue still lived nearby. We were together many weekends, sometimes back in her familiar house I'd loved as much as my own, and sometimes lost in exploration of my new apartment complex.

With Amy Sue nearby, it was as if everything hadn't ended for me. She was the connection, the link to all that was good and familiar and what might yet be. She was just "once removed," as we used to say, "from the real thing."

Then Mom fell in love.

"Yuk!" I told my diary and Amy Sue.

"Double yuk!" Amy Sue echoed, crossing her eyes and holding her nose.

This is a good thing, people tried to tell me.

43

But why didn't it feel that way? I asked my diary. Amy Sue said it just wasn't fair that kids had to do what adults told them to. "And they never even ask what we think about it."

Amy Sue was wise that way.

And then the final blow: another move, this time out of state.

New friendships were slow to form, the town strange. The new house we were building was unfinished, so we had to live in a dilapidated old place I was embarrassed for anyone to see, especially new kids. I didn't even want Amy Sue to see me living like this.

"If only," I wrote in my diary, "Mom hadn't made us move."

It became a familiar refrain even after we moved into our new house. It was too far out of town and now, as I complained to my mother, nobody would want to drive out this far to see me.

One particularly glum Friday, I walked down our wooded hill toward the house, thinking of what else I could tattle to diary about my mean old mother.

Mother greeted me at the door, her arms full of clean laundry. She loaded me down with shirts to hang in my closet and prodded me downstairs. She refused to argue when I protested about child labor, and she just laughed when I grumbled.

44

Still scowling, I opened my closet to hang up the shirts.

"Surprise!" Amy Sue yelled, jumping out and hugging me. "I'm here for the weekend. Your mom flew me over."

Forty years later, the memory of mother stashing my best friend in the closet still serves to ease the inevitable transitions that life brings. As I reread my diary, I realize now what I couldn't see then: that Mother did what she thought was best for the entire family, and that she was not—as I suspected at the time—immune to the pain it caused me.

Today is moving day again. This time for my mother, who's just moved into a retirement home.

Alone now, having lost her lifetime companion, my beloved stepfather, she needs someone to lift her spirits. That's why I'm picking up mother's best friend—Amy Sue's mom—at the airport and taking her to see an old friend.

Of Course She Knew

Ours is not a demonstrative family. When my mother was suffering from her final illness, I attempted several times to tell her how much I loved her, how much I was going to miss her, and what a good example she had been to me. She would gently wave away my words and change the subject, even though I couldn't help noticing that tears welled up in her eyes. "I hate good-byes," she told me more than once. "Let's not get dramatic."

I had to trust that she knew how I felt about her, even though she wouldn't let me show it in the usual way.

After the funeral, I—as the eldest daughter—took on the task of sorting through my mother's things. The last thing I went through was a trunk on the upper shelf of her bedroom closet. I suppose I put off going through it because I thought it might be full of old photos and letters from mother's girlhood that might bring on a fresh wave of tears.

What I found instead was a sort of informal biography of my own life. Inside the trunk was a lock of my baby hair, an envelope full of my baby teeth, a report card from kindergarten, and other such memorabilia, on up through pictures of my high school graduation and a napkin from my wedding reception.

What touched me most was to find every Mother's Day card I had ever given her in 33 years, from those with a crayon-scrawled "I love you," to the computer-generated, to the store-bought. As I tenderly flipped through these cards, reminiscing about the years that had slipped by so quickly, I knew not only that my mother loved me very much, but also that even without the words and hugs she found it so hard to accept, she had understood how very much I loved her back.

THE GOODNESS OF A HOME IS NOT DEPENDENT
ON WEALTH, OR SPACIOUSNESS, OR BEAUTY, OR LUXURY.
EVERYTHING DEPENDS ON THE MOTHER.

—*G.W.E. Russell*

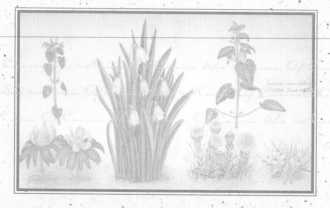

Philosophy 101

I was hit by a car when I was eight. I had been riding my bike home from the park after a game of kickball with the neighborhood kids, then, next thing I knew, I was in a hospital bed. I was in pretty bad shape the first weeks after I was hit, from what they tell me. I lay in a cast, unconscious, unresponsive. People told me later that everyone except my mother was preparing for "whatever happens." The likelihood was that I wouldn't survive.

I recall the faraway sound of my mother's voice saying patiently, "Remember, two times nine is eighteen. Three times nine is twenty-seven." And so she would proceed with the "ninesies" that I'd been struggling with before the accident put my life on hold. Multiplication tables had been the worst thing to happen to me in my short life . . . before the accident, of course.

Apparently undaunted by the maze of tubes and gadgets affixed to me, the grim prognosis, and my apparent disinterest in mathematics or waking up, Mother sat by my bed talking conversationally, saying her prayers, and then commencing with our lessons. Day after day, from the two-times to the twelve-times, she gave me questions and answers.

Doctors, nurses, even the rest of my family could barely conceal

their pity for her misguided energy. Still, she coached my unconscious self to focus, to try. Soon, Mother added books to the daily lessons. Science and space exploration had been my favorites, so she read aloud about galaxies, black holes, and space stations. At the end of each reading session, she stopped short of the conclusion, in hopes of sparking my curiosity...if it, indeed, had survived intact.

Somewhere between the rings of Saturn and life on Mars I began to stir. When, amazingly, I awoke, the doctors weren't sure if I would ever walk, talk, or ride a bike again. "Dependent," "invalid," and "limited" were words I overheard but didn't fully understand in my half-dazed state. More clear than the words of the doctors was the voice of my mother, whom I heard changing subjects, moving from multiplication and science to spelling.

49

"The spelling bee was your goal," Mother reminded, starting that very day with apple, aunt, and aardvark.

The morning after I spoke for the first time, she brought a globe to the hospital and started in on geography. State capitals, global exports, imports, customs. She asked the questions, took my face in her hands, looked into my eyes, and spoke the answer, pursing my lips to form the words for me.

I would like to say I was an attentive pupil, that I remember all this. How much I do and how much was told to me long after the fact, I can't be certain. I do know that as I lingered in that twilight valley of fear and doubt, it began to dawn on me that nobody would spend so much time on a kid who wasn't going to need to know this stuff. It was a turning point, awakening me to the possibility that I might indeed get better and have a "normal" life again. And if I did, I would still have to take math tests.

Days became months as I matched Mother's determination step for step. I completed all the "homework" she assigned me—easy stuff at first, like colors, shapes, and puzzles.

"You'll need to know this," Mother would say when I balked, "when you're an astronaut or an inventor or a rocket scientist. Remember what Shakespeare said: 'Readiness is all.'"

Mother and Shakespeare were right: In my job today as an

engineer, I need to know both the "ninesies" and geography. And I was ready—moving from the first difficult days back at school when numbers on a page were as undependable as my legs, to spelling bees, graduations, a successful career. Through it all, I've relied upon persistence, perseverance, and a deep belief that any goal is within reach, however far away it might seem. It's pretty obvious to me where I learned this philosophy: It took shape through the courage and dreams and will of a mother sitting beside a hospital bed, willing her hopes into reality.

Role Reversal

I know the exact moment it happened; the point at which my mom and I reversed our roles. It was the day my dad died. I was 55 years old, and my mom was 78. She called me from the hospital.

"It's Dad," she sobbed. "He's gone." My voice froze in my throat. She sounded like a little child—a lost little child.

"I'm coming, Mama," I cried out, swallowing my own grief. "I'll be right there."

As I made my way to the hospital, I remembered the many times she had been there to soothe away my hurts. Through each tragedy in my life, Mom had always been the great consoler, hugging me, stroking my hair, and whispering sweet words into my ear until I was ready to face the world again. Now it was my turn.

As I held her, I could feel how frail and thin she'd become after five years of caring for my dad. She was no longer the strong, capable person I had always known—the one who kissed away all hurts and had a solution for every problem. At this moment, she was the hurting child and I became the mother.

Over the next few weeks I did the things Mom would have done for herself if she could have—cooking, making funeral arrangements, and settling business affairs. She seemed so fragile and helpless, I soon began making plans to move her to my home.

It's been many years since Mom first came to live with me and my family. She's 92 now and thriving, and I'm still looking after her. In fact, I've been taking care of her almost as long as I've cared for my own children. I consider it a privilege after all she's meant to me.

I do for her the things she once did for me: I prepare her meals, launder her clothes, take her to the doctor and dentist, buy her pretty things to wear, and urge her to be as independent as possible. Now when we work together in the kitchen, I'm the one in charge and she's the helper. When she puts herself at risk, I do the scolding. And when she's ill, now I'm the one who worries and loses sleep.

Friends and acquaintances marvel at the things Mom is able to do at her age, and I can't help smiling like a proud parent. At times, I even find myself bragging about her accomplishments, just as she did when I was a child.

53

The First Thanksgiving

Her long-distance bill was going to be awful, Amy was sure, but she had so many questions! Her mom was back home in Arkansas, and here she was out in California, graduated from college and working at her first job. There wasn't time or money to fly home for Thanksgiving, and going to a restaurant sounded a little depressing. In a burst of brave ambition, she had decided to invite the few other single coworkers and neighbors she'd met in her first months in San Jose over to her apartment for a big, traditional holiday meal.

"Do you think I should grind up the cranberries, or would canned be good enough?" she asked her mother during one phone call, only to hang up and realize she still didn't know how many pounds of turkey it would take to feed six people. How long should it thaw? And where should she thaw it, for heaven's sake? She was sure her apartment-sized refrigerator wasn't big enough. She redialed the phone. Her mother recommended the cold-water-bath method of thawing it in the sink, constantly replenishing the ice cubes so it didn't spoil.

"I never knew this was so much work, Mom," Amy laughed. "I thought I was cooking a dinner, not running a Nordic spa!"

"It's not work, it's love," her mother replied. In Amy's colorful Southern family, food and love were inextricably tied. If a dish didn't turn out well, the cook would shake her head ruefully, lamenting, "I didn't love it enough."

It didn't help matters much that her mother's family used the oral tradition to pass recipes down through the generations. Nothing was written down.

Amy pushed speed-dial button number 1. "How much broth should I put in the stuffing?" she asked her mother.

"Hmmm." The telephone line hummed over the miles as her mom mulled this one over. "Just add it in a little bit at a time, darlin'," she finally answered in her slow drawl.

55

"But *about* how much?" Amy persisted.

Her mother was patient but stubborn. "I can't really answer that, sweetie. Just keep adding 'til it's right."

When Thanksgiving day dawned, Amy was up when the sky was still pewter, the telephone tucked firmly between her shoulder and her chin as her mother talked her through the basting and stuffing and browning like a faithful helper on a tech support line. The card tables Amy had carefully set up with candles and tablecloths looked lovely, if she did say so herself. Several of her guests brought delicious dishes. The meal went off without a hitch. A few even stayed to help wash up.

As the door closed behind the last guest to leave, Amy was already picking up the phone, her mood of exhilaration giving way to one of reflection. She'd pulled off a wonderful feast. Why hadn't it felt like a holiday? she wondered.

As she presented her triumphant, slightly homesick follow-up report to her mom, she heard the jumble of relatives' voices in the background and suddenly realized what had been missing from her celebration. There had been no cousins fighting over the wishbone, no day-long Monopoly game set up on the floor, where the dog had to be kept from running over the board and sending the pieces

flying. There had been no holding hands around the table before the meal, saying what each family member was most thankful for.

She knew then that learning to cook wasn't enough. She needed to develop her own traditions in order to make holidays meaningful in her own home, just as her mom had made them for her family. Her mom assured her that there was no magic recipe; all it would take was time. Like putting broth in the stuffing, Amy should just keep adding, "'til it's right."

***

SHE BROKE THE BREAD INTO TWO FRAGMENTS
AND GAVE THEM TO THE CHILDREN, WHO ATE WITH AVIDITY.
"SHE HATH KEPT NONE FOR HERSELF," GRUMBLED THE SERGEANT.
"BECAUSE SHE IS NOT HUNGRY," SAID A SOLDIER.
"BECAUSE SHE IS A MOTHER," SAID THE SERGEANT.

—*Victor Hugo*

Dandelion Dreams

G rowing up in Atlanta, I lived in a fancy neighborhood. It was enclosed by a black wrought-iron fence, and at the front gate there was a little gazebo where a gentleman in a green uniform checked people in and out. Everybody's yards were mowed the same height; flowers were chosen, arranged, and judged against a high standard; shrubs were kept pruned just so; and leaves were raked, bagged, and hauled away almost before they hit the ground by a service that came to the neighborhood in a pickup truck.

People driving along our street used to slow down and stare at the sweep of our manicured, green lawn and the carefully designed and tended flowers. We had the prize yard. It was like a painting, someone once told my mother. She was real pleased because she did most of the work herself. She spent hours on her hands and knees planting, weeding, trimming, fertilizing.

It was us, her kids—Toby, Patsy, and me—who caused our mother "...more trouble than a swarm of grasshoppers," as she used to say, rolling her eyes and sighing. It was probably true, because sometimes we forgot her rules and took shortcuts across the yard. That was a no-no. So was having a dog, which would surely leave spots on the grass and dig up her flowers. We couldn't have a

swingset either, or play ball on the lawn—same thing only worse: ruts and bare spots.

Mother wasn't really that fussy indoors, it was just something about her yard. "First appearances, you know. A yard makes a statement," she said. "People can tell right away what kind of family lives here."

This is why we couldn't believe our eyes when we came home from school one spring day and there, in our driveway, was a man unloading square logs from a truck. The kind of logs used to build playsets! The delivery man even left a fireman's pole, swings, and a climbing net in our driveway.

"It's high time there's some playing done in this fancy yard," said Mother.

We tried to be careful, but by the time the playset was built, the bare spots were already forming in the yard from where we'd started playing with the logs even before they were put up.

"Not to worry," Mother assured us, setting a picnic table on the velvety green grass within easy distance of the playset. It was so she could watch us and eat at the same time, she said. "And what about all the food we're likely to spill?" she asked. "Wouldn't a dog help clean up crumbs and crusts?"

We went with her and our father to the animal shelter and brought home a brown-and-white, long-tailed hound that immediately went to sleep under Mother's prize-winning dahlias, breaking some of the new stems.

"Not to worry," Mother said. "Puppies need their rest. After all, these are the 'dog days' of summer." Our father thought this was funny and laughed until he cried.

People were still driving past our house; sometimes they slowed, even stopped. But now they were saying to one another, "What is going on?"

"We're making a statement," Mother told one lady bold enough to ask, "about the kind of family that lives here. Let people talk, but tell them to send their kids on over," she said, hanging a dangling rope swing from the oak tree out back to seal her invitation.

"How about getting up a game of football with some of the neighbor kids?" Mother asked us that fall.

There was, she pointed out, plenty of room in the front yard. The azalea bushes could mark the goal lines at one end, the lilies could mark the other.

"Not to worry," she said when she saw the ruts and bare spots between the two. My father bought her a chaise lounge so she

could rest while she watched us play. Sometimes the dog lay there with her, both of them snoozing while we scored touchdowns in the gathering dusk.

It was useless to fertilize the lawn the next spring, what with its already ragged appearance. First base here, third there, home plate out by the roses. We'd become the designated neighborhood playground.

Now when people slowed to stare, they did so with raised eyebrows. My mother just waved from the chaise lounge where she spent most of her time now, laughing about the wonderful family that lived here and the statement it was making.

Drawn like moths to flame, neighborhood children continued to come, knowing they were not nuisances but welcome guests at the party of childhood thrown by my mother in her last year of life. She knew that life comes and goes faster than fluff on a dandelion.

Next time you're out driving and see a rutted yard overflowing with kids, toys, and maybe a funny old dog, you can bet that a mother loves there.

61

Happy Birthday to Me

World War II and I were born the same year. Although the war was over by my sixth birthday, it had left an indelible handprint upon my childhood. It was the hand that never had quite enough . . . enough money, enough food, enough clothes. And certainly it never held extras. Although the post-war South was recovering economically, the boom hadn't touched our family, which owned and operated a small printing business.

"We'll celebrate your birthday quietly this year," my mother explained, using a term that I didn't realize meant "frugally."

Skipping off to first grade that November day, I saw no problem with a quiet celebration. Quiet would be fine. So, at recess, I invited my entire class to come home with me for a party.

"A quiet party," I explained.

And there we went after school, 25 little kids following me, the birthday Pied Piper, fingers to our lips, whispering our way down the street.

My astounded mother, instead of scolding at the sight of a party-come-to-happen, thought quickly and acted even more quickly, frosting graham crackers, sticking candle stubs into six red apples, and leading the singing!

The quiet celebration? It was found in my mother's quick, easy welcome of the first graders who had come to enjoy a party.

"YOU ARE THE CARETAKER

OF THE GENERATIONS,

YOU ARE THE BIRTH-GIVER,"

THE SUN TOLD THE WOMAN.

"YOU WILL BE THE CARRIER

OF THIS UNIVERSE."

—*Sioux Sun Creation Myth*

63

Homecoming

"**I**'ve lost my daughter," stated the elderly lady who appeared at my desk in the newsroom. "And now I want to find her."

She stood there as if she were determined not to leave until she had my attention—and my help, if I got her meaning. The only clue to her nervousness was her hands, which were trembling inside white gloves. I'd not seen white gloves in years.

A lady from a bygone era, she had stopped by the daily newspaper where I was a reporter because, she explained, she needed help tracking down the daughter she'd released for adoption 50 years ago.

Time and changes of heart as well as circumstance had fanned her longing, she explained, and sparked her quest. I wasn't the first person she'd tried to enlist in her search. It had been going on for nearly five decades.

I was astounded. Nobody, I thought, sticks to anything that long in this instant-mashed-potato world of boredom, channel surfing, and throw-away moments.

"Will you help me find her?" she persisted.

The "how" of it remained vague, although I didn't have the heart to stop her as she began talking of that day long ago when she'd fallen victim to too many days of pregnancy without proper food and support and too many people willing only to point fingers without lifting one to help her. Ill and destitute, her back was to the wall in a borrowed one-room apartment when they came to put her in the hospital and take her baby. She was ill for months, and when she recovered and tried to reclaim her daughter, she found she was no longer entitled. The baby was gone. If she loved the baby, she was told, she would let the infant be adopted by a family who could take care of her. The implication of who *couldn't* take care of her was only too clear.

"A beautiful little girl," the woman told me now, time not lessening her heartbreak. "My parents made me sign the papers," she whispered. "There was no other way."

In time, she married a fine man who encouraged the search for her daughter. They'd had five children of their own, and he insisted that another one would be one more to love.

65

The empty spot in her heart would never be filled. She searched when she could, but with five children and a job, she had little concentrated time. And when she did, the official trail appeared to have been swept clean by fate—including a fire that had destroyed records, misspellings on the few documents she did find, and, above all else, a wall of massive indifference that greeted her.

"After my husband died a few years ago, I got the idea of going to newspapers near where I think my daughter might live. Maybe if you wrote a story..." her words trailed off as she saw the look of wariness on my face. I was thinking of legal entanglements, the time crunch this would create, the desire not to get involved in such a pathetic story.

And yet it wasn't pathetic. It was brave. Valiant. Even courageous. I tried to think what cause could be strong enough to propel me to visit every newspaper in a three-county area and essentially get down on my knees and beg bigshot reporter-types to help me. I drew a blank. Her stubbornness alone was worth a few lines of space in my column, and, after offering her a chair, I began making notes.

The following day, I ran a column essentially retelling her story. At the end of it I wrote, "... next Saturday is your birthday. Your mother asked that I send you this greeting: 'I've never stopped loving you. Each year, I bake you a birthday cake and sing to you.

The gift I gave you is letting you have a better life than you would have had with me. I hope and pray that it is still having many good returns. I love you.' If you read this," I added, "trust me, it's true."

There wasn't a dry eye in the readership, according to the letters I got the following week, but there were no leads. Interest dwindled as soon as something new drew people's short-lived attention.

Several days later, I looked up from my computer to see a plump, blond woman standing at my desk. "Can I help you?" I asked.

"I sure hope so," she said, holding out my column about the lost daughter. "You've got my mother."

Of course I had to write a follow-up story. But, though I am a wordsmith, I was at a loss for finding a way to describe their remarkable reunion. The word I finally settled upon was "homecoming." It had a very nice ring.

To Keith on His First Birthday

Dear Keith,

May 11, 1998

One year ago a nurse swaddled you in a blanket, handed you to me, and called you my son. You were beautiful and sweet and miraculous, with soft skin, a fuzzy patch of hair, eyes that looked vaguely like mine, and a wristband with information that matched the band around my wrist. You were a stranger.

Today, a year later, you are Keith Harris. And I'm your mom! We're best buddies, and we know each other well. Not only are you my son—you're you. Some of the most exciting moments of the past year have involved watching you reach the milestones that every baby reaches: the day you first sat up by yourself (October 4), the day your first two teeth came in (Christmas day), the first time you crawled (January 26). I'll never forget the pride I felt watching you face life's obstacles and master new skills. The most unforgettable times, though, have been smaller snapshots of your personality. When we filled

up your inflatable swimming pool for the first time, you jumped in without hesitation, laughing and squealing in delight despite the icy cold water, loving the fact that the sun was shining, you had a brand new, great big "bathtub" outside, and both your parents— your two favorite people—were there to watch you and play with you.

Every morning when I come into your room to get you from your crib, your eyes light up and your smile is the happiest, most genuine thing I've ever seen. It's almost as though you've forgotten over the course of the night how great life is and how much fun it is to see Mommy every day! This melts my heart almost as much as when I put you down to sleep at night, and you wrap your arms around my neck and lay your head on my shoulder, letting me know that after a game of peekaboo with Daddy, poking our heads in repeatedly for one last "Night, night, Daddy," you can't forget to give me my "Night, night" either.

There are just so many things I love about you, and I marvel at your wonderful qualities every day. I wish the world for you, as every parent does for their child, but mainly I wish the following things for you throughout your life:

• That you maintain your infectious sense of humor—everything makes you laugh and smile, and that's the most important quality I can think of in a person who enjoys and appreciates life.

69

• That you continue to savor new experiences and approach challenges with concentration, excitement, and good humor.

• That you are surrounded by family and friends who love you and whom you love right back with everything you've got (just like now).

I also hope you eventually find a career that challenges your abilities and fulfills your dreams as well as a family that makes you as happy as mine makes me. But for now, I hope you have a fantastic, unforgettable childhood, and I promise I will do everything I can to make that a reality.

I love you, love you, love you.

Mom

No Matter What

Monday dawned a waiting day. Cold, a light snow, sharp northerly wind. I shivered in the chill of winter. Or maybe the shiver was because I felt nervous.

Today was the Big Day.

I had an appointment with the board of education to interview for a teaching position—a position for which I'd studied and trained for months, and had finally applied for several weeks earlier. I was willing to start anywhere, even in the most lowly assignment at the most difficult school on the outskirts of our town.

This was the Great Depression, and jobs were almost as scarce as optimism.

I took a deep breath, pulled the brim of my hat down firmly, and set off for the interview, trying to think positive thoughts and hoping I looked more capable than my young years implied.

* * *

When I returned home late that afternoon, bursting with excitement, the dining room table was set with Mother's finest china and crystal, candles and a single pink rose in a cut-glass vase made a lovely centerpiece on her "company" lace tablecloth. My

younger brothers and sisters had been scrubbed until they practically shone. I smelled what had to be chicken and dumplings cooking in the kitchen. And could that be the aroma of a peach cobbler wafting this way?

My good news paled beside this feast.

At dinner, I found a carefully printed card in Mother's looping handwriting tucked beneath my dinner plate.

Congratulations! I knew you would get the job. This special meal tonight and our very best things show you how much I love you and how proud we all are of you. Love, Mother.

It was a truly celebratory feast. But how had my mother known I got the job, I wondered all through the meal. Perhaps, I finally decided, someone from the

school board had called me at home, with some new information about my position, tipping off Mother.

It wasn't until Mother got up to clear the dishes from the table to make way for dessert, which was indeed peach cobbler, that I understood. As she carried the dirty dishes through the swinging door into the kitchen, a second note fell from her dress pocket.

I picked it up and read it.

Don't feel too bad about not getting the job today, it said. Another opportunity will turn up. You deserve the best that life has to offer. This special meal and our very best things show you how much I love you and how proud we all are of you. Love, Mother.

To Mother, I was a success no matter what. And it is that "no matter what" that has sent me back out the door time and again over the years with my head held high and a sense of confidence that I will succeed.

The Best New Year's Eve Party Ever

At the most memorable New Year's Eve party I ever went to, there were no noisemakers, no bottles of champagne, and no silly hats. And though my green gown was fashionably backless, I certainly wasn't dressed in style.

The reason, you see, was that I went into labor on the last day of the old year. That afternoon, amidst the high-tech machines and monitors of the delivery room, the hustle and bustle of the nurses, and my ragged breathing, with my husband by my side whispering encouragement and holding my hand, I gave birth to our first child.

Our little family spent New Year's Eve in the hospital, celebrating the new year with a new life. The party consisted of my husband, myself, and our tiny, perfect newborn. Occasionally the party was crashed by a nurse who came in to take my blood pressure.

Exhausted and indescribably happy, my husband and I toasted each other with grape juice as we planned the wonderful year to come. We didn't resolve to lose weight or get more exercise or paint the kitchen, only to do for this incredibly beautiful baby the very best that we could. We didn't even manage to stay up until midnight. Dick Clark had to count the old one out and the new one in without us. Still, it was the best New Year's Eve party any of us will ever have.

Round the idea of one's mother, the mind clings with

fond affection. It is the first thought

stamped upon our infant hearts,

when yet soft and capable of receiving

the most profound impressions . . . all after feelings

are more or less light in comparison.

I do not know that even in our old age we

do not look back to that feeling

as the sweetest we have ever known. . .

—*Charles Dickens* (1812–1870), *from* All Year Around

Thanks for the Cookies, Mom

Ginny sat alone in her living room, staring at the clock. In just a few moments, Chad's frigate, loaded with supplies, weapons, and several hundred men, would put out to sea, leaving its safe berth in the San Diego sun. Military regulations forbade her son from writing his exact itinerary. All Ginny knew was that her 18-year-old son, looking terribly adult in his sailor suit, would travel farther and faster than she had in her entire life, before sailing up a hazardous finger of water in the mid-East.

Mainly to divert her thoughts and keep herself busy, Ginny headed for the kitchen. She filled her island countertop with flour, sugar, spices, eggs, and her largest bowls and utensils. By the time she had exhausted herself, dozens of cookies covered nearly every surface.

Dividing them into three batches, Ginny wrapped some to bring to her neighbors, put a portion in the freezer, and then carefully double-wrapped and secured a box for Chad. She lettered his new F.P.O. address atop the lid and headed for the post office.

"Chad may have just left, but he'll know how much I miss him when

these arrive," she said, to nobody in particular.

The cookies were a hit with her son and his shipmates, despite the fact that they all arrived broken. "The guys loved 'em anyway," he wrote, "and we ate them all in less than an hour. Can you make ginger snaps next time?"

Determined to make sure they arrived whole, Ginny tried a different wrapping technique the next time she mailed her cookies. She had read somewhere that popcorn makes an excellent shipping cushion, so she popped a huge batch, then tucked the cookies inside.

"Hey, Mom, do you think you could put some salt on the popcorn next time?" Chad wrote innocently. "It was kind of dry, but we ate it anyway. What a surprise to find cookies in the box! Thanks from all of us—especially John, who loves ginger snaps. Any chance of peanut butter cookies next time?"

Ginny happily filled the request, sliding the soft peanut butter cookies into cardboard potato chip sleeves, then double boxing them. Every cookie arrived in one piece, Chad happily reported. Sadly, the cookies were so moist they developed mold en route.

"We wiped it off and ate them anyway, Mrs. Baxter," read the note signed by Chad and five of his shipmates. "And, no, we didn't get sick," the postscript added.

So went Ginny's odyssey of baking, refining recipes, packing, shipping, critiquing, and waiting. With each cookie shipment, the number of signatures on Chad's letters grew. At Christmastime, Ginny found herself packing 20 tiny, silk Christmas trees in tubes and sending them out along with box after box of holiday candy, cookies, and cakes. "I think I've adopted an entire ship," she laughed, placing the crate on the post office counter with a thud.

The months passed, and Ginny kept baking. It seemed like every day when the mail carrier arrived, he delivered at least one chatty, friendly letter from one of the sailors, thanking her for the treats. The first notes she received were addressed "Dear Mrs. Baxter." As time went on, the greetings evolved into "Hello Mrs. B," "Dear Ginny," then, one day, Ginny grinned in delight when she opened a letter from one of Chad's friends and read "Hi Mom!"

Eventually, Ginny received word the ship was returning home. She smiled, considering the hundreds of pounds of cookies she had baked over the last few months. Wondering

who had benefitted the most from her kitchen frenzy—the shipful of young men or her own psyche—she realized it didn't matter. What mattered was the way she was going to miss the dozens of young men she had never even met. As their unofficially appointed cookie-baking Mom, she decided to rectify that. She made arrangements to be at the port when the ship arrived.

* * *

As the ship sailed into the bay, the sailors observed tradition by lining up in their whites on the dock. Standing amid hundreds of excited friends and family, Ginny almost bounced up and down in excitement at the thought of seeing Chad again. The prospect of finally meeting all of her new friends was almost as exciting to her. As the ship inched its way into the dock, with Ginny straining to catch her first glimpse of Chad, she noticed a huge banner held up by what appeared to be the entire front line of men. "Thanks for the cookies, Mom!" it read. "They were great!"

GOD COULD NOT BE EVERYWHERE,
AND THEREFORE HE CREATED MOTHERS.

—*Jewish proverb*

The Pin

When I was young, the general store cast a powerful spell over me. Upon those dusty, crammed shelves sat pleasure, temptation, and, once, my heart's desire.

A glass-enclosed candy display presented the main attraction for kids. Beyond that finger-smudged barrier lay a confectionary wonderland. I lingered over my favorites, choosing from caramel pinwheels, lemon drops, and chocolate kisses and passing over peppermint sticks, licorice strings, and root beer barrels. All transactions were contemplated deeply. One for a penny or two for a penny was a tough choice.

Summertime brought miniature wax soda bottles filled with a swallow of sweet liquid and tiny candy ice-cream cones topped with sugar-sprinkled marshmallow. I enjoyed these all summer long, then licked my lips as Halloween approached and candy corn and wax teeth took their place.

I was eight and, on a casual browse through the merchandise room, I saw something that stopped me in my

tracks. Fastened to a small square of white cardboard, high on a shelf where nothing could happen to it, sat the most beautiful piece of jewelry I had ever seen. I stood transfixed as my friends moved on, and I studied the details of the pink-and-white rhinestone flower upon a golden stem. Though not exactly the pearl of great price, to a third grader rhinestones were close enough. I had to have it. At the time, I had never heard of layaways or buying on time. I just left everything to chance and started saving my money.

I gazed at my pin while my friends conducted business over the penny candy. No gumdrops for me, no butterscotch, either. Every penny I had was carefully socked away in my piggy bank and taken out every night to be counted. The price of the piece of jewelry amounted to less than a dollar, but when measured in chocolate drops and coconut strips, it seemed impressive.

Red-and-white striped candy canes and chocolate Santas had replaced Halloween fare when I finally exchanged my pennies, nickels, and dimes for the pin I coveted. The proprietor smiled as I carefully counted out my change. If she had noticed my daily pilgrimages to the jewelry counter, she never said, but her smile, as she wrapped the pin in tissue and handed it over, was tender.

I was once again free to indulge my sweet tooth to my heart's content. I had discovered, however, something sweeter than all the candy I had sacrificed. At Christmas there would be a special package under our tree. Inside would be the prettiest pin I had ever seen, and the tag would say, "For my mom."

◦◦◦◦◦

THERE NEVER WAS A WOMAN LIKE HER.

SHE WAS GENTLE AS A DOVE

AND BRAVE AS A LIONESS . . . .

THE MEMORY OF MY MOTHER AND HER

TEACHINGS WERE THE ONLY CAPITAL

I HAD TO START LIFE WITH,

AND ON THAT CAPITAL I HAVE MADE MY WAY.

—*Andrew Jackson*

From Mom to Mom

The day before I delivered Anna, I thought I was *sooooo* ready. I was tired of looking like a cargo van, I was over the adorableness of waddling, and the fact that I couldn't see my feet was getting on my nerves.

Even in the hospital, after the last-minute caesarean section, I continued to believe I had everything under control. Of course, it escaped me that the nurses and doctors were doing all the difficult stuff. The only real responsibilities I had were feeding Anna and getting myself strong. Oh yes, I also had the grand duty of greeting visitors, eating chocolate gifts they brought, and accepting warm compliments for this perfect newborn I had created.

It wasn't until I left the hospital that I realized how totally unready I really was. In a sheer panic, I listened to my daughter cry and wondered why no one was doing anything to quiet her. With complete confusion, I watched her feed and thought, "Say something, Anna. Are you full now? Do you want more?"

83

Anna's daddy was no less perplexed. He mostly just paced back and forth and repeatedly offered to get my mom, who was spending a week in my guest room, ready to help out if needed.

At first my mom's help wasn't easy to pinpoint. It was all so unassuming. She would come into the room, gently shift her daughter's arms while adjusting her granddaughter's head, and suddenly the feeding process worked. In the wee hours of the night, she would quietly stand in the threshold of my bedroom and wait patiently as Anna nursed. If I pulled it off, Mom quietly retreated back to the guest room. Other times, when sweat formed on my brow and my baby's mouth went every place but where it should be, Mom slowly, silently made some minor modifications, then went back to bed.

When Anna was just two days old, Mom went home. "But you said you'd stay the week," I pleaded.

"You can do it," she replied, waving as she rode away. But when I called three hours later, desperate for information on how to bathe an infant, she returned. While she soaped Anna, I watched from behind. "Babies love their bath," Mom explained. "Just support the head and shoulders so they feel secure." Then she dried her granddaughter and left. When I called two hours later, hysterical because my daughter was hysterical, she returned. While she held Anna close and paced the full length of our house, I watched from

behind. "Most babies have a fussy hour," Mom explained, "You just have to walk it out. There's nothing wrong." When her grand-daughter stopped crying, she left.

At first I thought my mom was dotty. Why didn't she just stay all week like she promised? My SOS calls grew farther apart, however. I began actually applying some of my mother's advice. Eventually I realized that I could never become a mom like my mom if no one gave me a chance. My mom, ever near in the wings, was giving me a chance. That's when I learned my most important lesson about motherhood: a lesson that would be important when Anna turned one month and equally important when Anna had her own baby.

A mother has to teach and then retreat. A child of any age needs time to explore her own strengths. This bit of insight was the nicest baby gift anyone gave me.

The Dance of Comrades

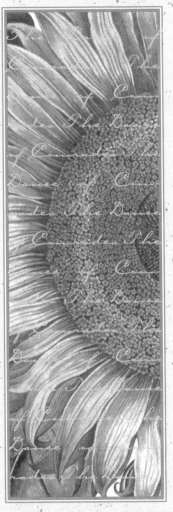

Braving the crescendo of music blaring through Jeremy's door, I braced myself, opened the door a crack, and peeked in. Jeremy had fallen asleep, nail-bitten fingers splayed on his pillow. Sleep had erased his earlier tension.

Tension seemed to be growing between us as quickly as the barely visible "caterpillar" that sprouted on his upper lip. I resisted an urge to straighten his desk, crowded with homework, the latest CDs, and sports magazines. I turned down the stereo, stilling its frenzied message that seemed to herald Jeremy's entry into adolescence.

Clicking off the lamp, I sat down for a minute in his old rocker. I had refinished it to a satin touch during my last awkward weeks of pregnancy 13 long years ago. I had been too excited and impatient to sit still that long-ago fall as I pictured the baby growing inside me and dreamed of the person it would become.

"*I love you*," I'd whispered, as I lovingly resanded and recaned the splintered seat, weaving into it affection for the child already straining against my motherly restrictions.

We had been close from the start. I rocked him through many restless nights, crooning lullabies composed from my determination all would be well in his life. Our bond had grown even stronger over the years, a tie forged by necessity after my divorce.

"Comrades," he'd called us.

Not comrades today, I thought sadly, remembering our latest fight of the afternoon.

"What a wimp," he'd wailed, hating the freckles dusting his nose, the stubborn cowlick. Spending hours in front of the mirror, he could only focus on the day's single pimple, certain to "ruin everything."

"Why did you let me start kindergarten so early?" he accused. "I'm the youngest, shortest kid in my class." He was torn between hiding in his room until he grew or straining his muscles and my patience as he lifted weights and consumed pounds of "body-building food." While he was waiting for the transformation, cryptic slang and disgracefully tattered clothes lent him invisibility, helping him blend into the crowd. His uncertainties were so intense they touched me even in the midst of our fights.

87

He would be what my mother had once called me—a "late bloomer." I'd tried to explain the concept to Jeremy, telling him about David, the late bloomer whose last name followed mine on classroom rosters. Shorter than me by several inches, David had loved me from afar just as I, in turn, hankered after those beyond my reach. David was now a tall, handsome, successful actor, resplendent in full flower. At our class reunion, he'd retained only his smile to identify him.

"You don't understand," Jeremy had told me, an accusation he shouted at least a dozen times a day in a voice sliding up and down the emotional scale.

The very words, I was suddenly stung into recalling, I'd flung at my own mother years ago! I brought the rocking chair to a halt, tilting the kaleidoscope of memory to bring the past into sharper focus. Though I'd forgotten until now, my disguise of confidence had been triple-fold bobby sox and swishing, swinging crinoline skirts as a child of the '50s! Bop bop a lu bop, sham bam boo! There was the answer, the bridge Jeremy and I could cross. Laughing is better than fighting, I thought, rising from the rocker, even if I'm the punch line.

* * *

When Jeremy came downstairs for breakfast the next morning, he found my high school yearbooks stacked beside his cereal bowl.

One was propped open. I'd spent hours last night hunting through the attic until I found them.

I pointed to the opened yearbook and casually asked, "Recognize anybody?"

There I was, a wide, bright yellow streak of peroxide running through my hair, staring rebelliously from the page. As my mother had predicted, my bleached stripe had lasted much longer than the fad. "You don't understand," I'd tried to tell her before sneaking away to do the bad hair deed. Ah, but she had, I realized now.

Jeremy stared incredulously at the photo, swung his gaze back to me, and then looked back at the yearbook. He started to giggle uncontrollably.

"Jeremy, have I ever told you about the time when I..." I began, swinging my foot in long-forgotten jitterbug patterns, as my son and I slowly but surely resumed the dance of comrades.

89

The Greatest Fan

Now that I'm a mother, schlepping kids to softball or soccer, football or ballet, I sometimes wonder where my life went. I barely remember an existence without my back end cradled in a vinyl bucket seat, hands gripping the wheel, voice straining to be heard above the clamor, "Now, who needs to be where first?"

It's times like these I remember my original thoughts on parenthood—lazy afternoons in the garden with my kids ... tea parties in the playroom ... pleasant family meals on our back porch. Not even close! But as I watch my zeal for motherhood speed down Carpooler's Highway #1, I do at least experience a new admiration for my own mom—at last.

As a girl, I never appreciated my mother's constant presence at all my games, at every science fair, at every school production. Was she wanting to be off with the ladies-who-lunch? Did she long for pretty afternoons on the golf course? Did I ever say

thank you to her for giving up every spare moment to schlep me around, then stay until the very end of whatever activity was on that day's agenda? Did I ever even realize she was my most ardent fan? No, I don't think so. I think I'll call and thank her today. Of course, I'll have to call from the car phone, because I don't see a schlepping break any time soon.

THERE'S ONLY ONE PRETTY CHILD IN THE WORLD,
AND EVERY MOTHER HAS IT.

—*Cheshire proverb*

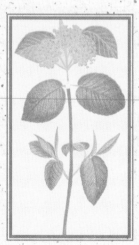

Letters from Camp Jericho

I *Hate It Heer,* the first letter read. That was all. And beneath the word "heer," Jeremy had scrawled both his first and last names, in letters large enough to fill the entire page, to be sure his parents knew the identity of the writer.

Marge looked at Sam tearfully. "He hates it there," she said, overcome by a great wash of guilt.

"He'll get over it," Sam answered gently, scanning the Dow-Jones with a frown meant for the market. "Everyone hates camp at first. It's perfectly normal."

I reely hate it heer. We got snakes. Giant rats. Alegators. And the cownslors are meen!!! Jeremy's second letter reported. Marge envisioned a Caribbean penal colony with children shackled to trees. Despite Sam's attempts to reassure her, Marge was convinced this wasn't "normal."

Dialing the camp's phone number, Marge demanded to speak to John Jamieson. A seasoned camp owner, he suspected the reason for

the call. "Mrs. Stark, there are no snakes, giant rats, or alligators here," he assured her. "You toured our facility. This isn't the Everglades. Jeremy is an imaginative little boy and very homesick . . . like most first-time campers."

"He's miserable," Marge countered. "What can we do?"

"Trust me. He's going to be fine." Jamieson responded kindly. "Give him another week. In the meantime, just keep writing to him and urging him to have fun."

From the moment she hung up the phone, Marge realized she needed to do more than write letters. But what would it take to show Jeremy how much he was loved and missed? That's when she decided to start her "Love of the Day" campaign. Every day she would mail something fun to make him feel special. The plan lifted her heart and made her feel almost cheery.

From the start, her plan worked its own special magic. When she mailed Jeremy his favorite stuffed bear, she got an immediate response. *Wow! Thanks for sending Ted,* Jeremy wrote, in normal-sized letters. *He's on my bunk and sometimes I take him to swim class.* Conspicuously missing were the words *I hate it heer.*

93

Marge mailed a big tin of his favorite jelly beans with instructions to share with his bunkmates. *Yore the greatest!!!!!!* the next postcard announced. *My frends want you for there mom. Love, Jeremy.*

A photo of the entire family taken the previous summer found its way into a cardboard frame Marge decorated by pressing Noodles' paw onto an ink pad. The gift and "note" from the cat were a big hit. *Camp is cool,* Jeremy pronounced, *and you are, too.*

With each passing day, Marge felt more confident. She found she could go to work and actually concentrate on her job, and she and Sam enjoyed their time alone together enormously. The time flew by, and Parent Day at Camp Jericho was upon them. Marge looked and felt more relaxed than she had in ages.

"Honey, I've got to hand it to you," Sam said. "Your 'Love of the Day' plan was brilliant. I never thought I'd be saying this, but part of me hoped Jeremy would be too homesick to stick it out. I've missed him more than I ever imagined!"

The two drove through the gate, catching sight of a porch full of excited children. Jeremy, whom Marge swore had grown a foot, waved and shouted. As soon as the car came to a halt, he ran down the steps into Marge's outstretched arms.

"C'mon, Mom!" he shouted. "I want to show you my bunk . . . and these are my friends . . . and wait 'til you see what I made . . ." he

babbled, dragging her along. He didn't let go of Marge's hand until they reached his cabin, where he proudly showed off his collection of "Love of the Day" memorabilia.

"I'm ready to rename this place Camp Marge Stark," John Jamieson confided, escorting the couple to lunch in the newly redecorated dining hall. "Just between us, Jeremy was about the most homesick kid I've seen in years, and I had my doubts about whether he'd stick it out. Your miracle turned him around. I've shared it with some other parents, and they think you're a genius." Marge giggled with pleasure, stepping into the dining hall.

Catching her breath, Marge stopped short. On the wall, giant, hand-painted murals of wildlife filled the room with color. Over the serving area, a giant, silly-looking alligator in a Camp Jericho cap posed with an equally comical raccoon as red, green, and blue snakes dangled from trees.

We got snakes. Giant rats. Alegators, Marge recalled with a grin. And to think she'd been worried about him!

95

Hidden Thorns

When I turned 12, Mom made sure I had exactly what I wanted for my birthday: a party at the local pizza palace, a couple of electronic games, and a pair of roller skates. Mom made sure to get my younger sister a pair, too, so there would be no arguments.

I found great freedom in those skates. After getting accustomed to them, my sister and I rode several times around the block on our new wheels. Before long, I became bored with the easy path we were taking, so I chose something more exciting.

I decided to skate down a neighbor's steep drive and into the street. I knew it was dangerous, but it was precisely that element of danger that I craved. I told my sister to watch for cars while I readied myself at the top.

After making two exhilarating trips down the drive, I stood poised for one last time before switching places with her. I could feel the October breeze dancing jigs in my hair.

"Go!" she shouted.

I felt a rush of wind in my face as I leapt into action. Pushing forward on one foot, then the other, I gathered speed. Without any warning, my sister suddenly yelled, "Wait! There's a car coming!"

At that moment, I had only two choices: skate down the drive into the path of an oncoming car or swerve into the rosebush-lined fence. Certain death or merely big-time pain. I chose the latter. Bracing for the impact, I slammed into the fence, feeling the sting of each thorn that jabbed my hands and arms. I howled in pain as I skated the rest of the way down the drive and raced toward home.

I skated onto my patio, where my mother sat reading the evening newspaper. Tears streaked my face. Between sobs, I told her what had happened. She calmly unlaced my skates and sat me down while she went inside for tweezers.

97

For about an hour that day, Mom patiently pulled those thorns, one by one, from my arms and hands. "I never saw the thorns, Mom," I said, hoping she wouldn't be mad.

She paused a moment and looked directly at me. Then she said something I wouldn't fully understand until many years later. "Sweetheart, there are plenty of thorns in this life," she told me. "Just don't forget how sweet the roses are."

To this day, I haven't forgotten.

———◦◦◦———

I SHALL NEVER FORGET MY MOTHER,
FOR IT WAS SHE WHO PLANTED AND NURTURED
THE FIRST SEEDS OF GOOD WITHIN ME.
SHE OPENED MY HEART TO THE IMPRESSIONS OF NATURE;
SHE AWAKENED MY UNDERSTANDING
AND EXTENDED MY HORIZON, AND HER
PERCEPTS EXERTED AN EVERLASTING INFLUENCE
UPON THE COURSE OF MY LIFE.

—*Immanuel Kant*

Potpourri

I would need to stop and count how many places I lived before I was 15 years old. My family moved at least a dozen times because of Father's job. That's a lot of schools to survive, new faces to learn, and towns and neighborhoods to navigate. My two brothers and two sisters and I kept pretty busy.

Contrary to what you might think, those were some of the happiest days of my life. I still write to several of the scattered friends I made all those years ago and consider many of the small towns where we lived my "hometown."

That's not to say we kids didn't feel sad when moving day came. We did. But we knew we wouldn't feel like strangers for long, thanks to our mother and her "welcome" gifts. These gifts weren't given to us; they were given by us.

Mother, a small woman with laugh lines permanently etched around her eyes and mouth, didn't wait for

others to approach us when we moved in; she led the way. With five kids traipsing along behind her like ducks in a row, she made her way up and down the streets of our newest neighborhood.

At each home, Mother introduced herself and us and offered the lady of the house a small sachet of homemade potpourri.

"I always keep a batch going," she would explain. "Herbs and flowers, bits of this and that given to us by the people in all the places we've lived so I'll not soon be forgetting them." And then she named them. The places did sound exotic when spoken in her Scottish brogue; our family seemed brave in her telling. Sometimes Mother and the new neighbor would discover a place or a person in common. Strangers suddenly became near-kin when that happened!

Mother ended each stop by inviting each new acquaintance to come visit and have a cup of tea and, if they wanted, to bring along a wee bit of something to add to her "friendship pot" as she called it, urging them also to bring their children and husbands along.

And people did. They brought all sorts of interesting things—flowers, herbs, or petals from their gardens, and spices from their kitchen. Other people brought scraps of material or lace to make sachet covers as well as carefully ironed ribbons with which to tie them. The most important thing they brought, however, was the gift that Mother first extended to them: friendship between strangers.

It was, to my mind at least, no coincidence that Mother's name was Rosemary, the herb of remembrance.

DEAR MOTHER: I'M ALL RIGHT. STOP WORRYING ABOUT ME.

—*Egyptian papyrus letter, circa 2000 B.C.*

Home Sweet Unusual Home

If kindergarten had been hard for Jenny, first grade was going to be harder, I thought, as I watched my daughter playing in the backyard. All summer Jenny had worried about first grade, speaking nostalgically about kindergarten and with absolute reverence about preschool. First grade loomed less than two weeks away.

"Sitting in a desk all day, eating lunch at school. Staying out of the big kids' way." And with that, she would begin to cry.

"Change is hard," I'd told her lamely. "You'll do fine."

And she would. Could, I amended. She was bright, capable, and at times excited about learning to read and do "add ups," as she called mathematics. If only she could believe she had the courage to make the leap from here to there. This wouldn't be the first time, I realized, that my daughter and I would disagree about her abilities.

It was clear that neither my wishing nor my platitudes were working. Time for drastic measures.

* * *

While Jenny was at her swimming lesson, I cruised the alleys of our town until I found what I wanted behind the appliance store. Someone had bought a new refrigerator, leaving behind its cardboard box like a crab does its shell when it moves to a larger one.

A home for Jenny.

I convinced the appliance store guy to give me the box. "Empty?" he asked several times, just for clarification.

"For now," I said, my voice strong with more hope than conviction. But, I figured, for centuries mothers have invented quilts from scraps, meatloaf from hamburger, and casseroles from leftovers. I could surely wing it for now.

It was all I'd hoped for and more, the meeting of Jenny and the box.

"Can I have it?" she asked, hopping on one foot and then the other.

"I got it for you," I said, careful not to direct its use.

By supper time, Jenny had dragged the box into her bedroom, already crowded with a play kitchen, bookshelves, scattered toys. I swallowed my suggestion that the box live on the porch where I'd envisioned it. Jenny wanted it nearby, adding it to her familiar clutter.

By bedtime, Jenny had marked where she wanted me to cut a door and windows. She colored them silver, blue, and pink. An oatmeal box, painted red, made a tip-tilted but serviceable chimney; shoe boxes were more than adequate window boxes.

Jenny fell asleep facing the box and, for the first time in days, didn't awaken with a bad dream about getting lost hunting for her first-grade classroom.

With the morning, Jenny resumed homemaking. Into the house went dolls, books, blanket. She secured it all with a ring of old keys, putting them in her dress-up purse each time she left home.

"Jenny's Hom," read the sign she carefully printed with bold strokes of crayon and glitter. When I gently suggested an "e" be added to her sign, she asked if "home" was a word you learn in first grade.

"Probably," I hedged, making a mental note to tell her new teacher to please let it be!

"I want to eat lunch in my house, Mama," Jenny said, appearing at my elbow in the kitchen.

Cheese-triangle sandwiches, raisins, milk in a dolly tea set. "Mmmm, good," she smiled her appreciation.

So few things, I thought as I delivered her popsicle dessert, are seen from a child's-eye viewpoint, for they are outnumbered, over-

shadowed, and dwarfed by the gigantic trappings of our adult world.

In a cardboard home, in a fairy-tale forest, in a land beyond, Jenny has taken up residence away from home for the first time. A safe first move, she in the middle of her own room with Mom in the kitchen, as far away as she needed me to be.

Sometimes I went for tea, even though only part of me fit in her home with an "e."

"You can eat on my porch," invited this precious child, who was already moving us toward places I can never follow.

* * *

Tomorrow is the first day of school. Jenny had her new clothes ready—down to a matching hair bow. After brushing her teeth, she snuggled into the nest she'd made inside her box. I sat outside its "door" and listened to her excited, only slightly apprehensive chatter. Gradually her voice slowed as she drifted to sleep. And still I sat, listening to her soft snoring inside her home away from home, a first step on the path into the rest of her life. She could live in it until she outgrew it . . . and her worries. I was reassured knowing that Jenny would always know when and where to go next.

Day of Reckoning

I remember well the day of the big storm. I had just gotten home from school and had dived into my afternoon snack when I noticed the blue sky turn a greenish-gray. Storms popped up all the time near our house, but this one seemed different.

"Mom," I hollered, "there's a storm coming!" I heard a mumble of agreement from her studio. I knew she was busily putting the final brush strokes on a watercolor for her latest exhibit.

I shouted once more. "Mom, did you hear what I said?" Silence greeted me. When she was at work, she didn't seemed to know that I existed. It seemed as if those paintings were all she cared about.

A shuddering thunderclap above our house finally roused Mom from her studio. The wind was shrieking outside, and I watched jagged streaks of lightning rip through the sudden blackness. I jumped as thunder cracked again, this time so loud it must surely be right outside the window.

Mom appeared at my side. Was that a look of worry on her face? I couldn't be sure, because with the next bolt of lightning the power went out and the entire house went dark. Mom grabbed me in her arms and raced downstairs to the basement. The rain pounded the

roof, slamming in sheets against the basement windows. Mom grabbed a blanket and threw it around us, and we huddled in a corner of our makeshift shelter.

Upstairs, we could hear things crashing. I could hear Mom's paintings hit the floor, one by one, and I felt her stiffen as each one fell. With every crash, her hand faltered, then she resumed stroking my hair.

Much later, after the wind died down, we ventured from our hiding place. We were shocked at what we saw. We could see daylight peeking through where a piece of roof had been ripped off. In the living room, it looked as if a giant hand had reached in and picked up our furniture, snapping it into pieces and scattering them all over. Outside, several of our trees were downed, and our car was flipped onto its side.

When we looked into Mom's studio and found almost all of her beloved paintings ruined, I was filled with sorrow. I knew how much her paintings meant to her, and I knew this had to be the most devastating loss of all. I started to tell her how sorry I was, but before I had a chance, Mom leaned down and kissed my forehead, then squeezed me so tight I could barely breathe. At that moment, I finally realized what my mother considered most precious.

Nature Beckons

hat a relief to see the sun again after a week of rain. It seemed like I'd been cooped up in the house with my bored six-year-old for a month.

"Come on, Adam," I said, grabbing his hand, "let's go for a walk." Walking toward a wooded area, we chatted about how fresh the day smelled. In the woods, I sat on a rock while Adam plopped down on a stump. As I drank in the refreshing air, he examined a pine sapling.

"Look, Adam," I said, touching a small tree, "one day this will be as big as those." I pointed to the top of the tallest pine I could find. He craned his neck to see. "How do they get that big, Mom?"

"It's simple, they grow up." I tousled his blonde hair. "Just like you will."

"You mean I'll be as big as Dad one day?"

"Yes, Son," I said, "maybe even bigger."

Watching his face, I saw skepticism in his wrinkled nose and raised eyebrow. Then belief dawned as he contemplated this incredible information, which must be true because it had come from me.

* * *

It's been 12 years since we took that walk, but my son still talks about all the times we spent out in the woods, sharing, talking, "growing up." Today, at 6'1", he's a full head taller than his father. But still, whenever he has something to talk about, he says, "Mom, let's go for a walk."

———❖———

THERE WAS A PLACE IN CHILDHOOD
THAT I REMEMBER WELL
AND THERE A VOICE OF SWEETEST TONE
BRIGHT FAIRY TALES DID TELL
AND GENTLE WORDS,
AND FOND EMBRACE
WERE GIVEN WITH JOY TO ME
WHEN I WAS IN THAT HAPPY PLACE
UPON MY MOTHER'S KNEE.

—*Samuel Lover*

109

My New Mom

T he wedding was perfect. Glorious weather. The caterer outdid herself. The tent sparkled with Italian lights, and Emily felt like a princess. When she stepped onto the red carpet she knew all her planning had paid off.

"I'm glad we hired a videographer," Emily said as she and Aaron enjoyed their first dance as husband and wife. "I'd never be able to remember it all otherwise!"

Aaron held her tightly, studying her eyes. "No glitches?"

"Not one," she grinned as the music ended and the cart with the wedding cake was rolled onto the dance floor. Emily's mom, in characteristic style, raced out with a makeup bag and powdered Emily's nose. The photographer began snapping away as Aaron "accidentally" missed Emily's mouth while feeding her cake, decorating her face with icing.

"Let me get that!" Betty offered, producing a tissue. Emily's new mother-in-law tucked her hair behind her ear and tenderly cupped her face. "I'm thrilled you're my daughter at last," she smiled. "I'd be honored if you'd call me mom."

The request took Emily aback. For years, Betty had been "Mrs. Abbott." The thought of calling her "Mom" was unsettling, but Emily wasn't sure why. Sensing her hesitation, Betty patted her hand and smiled. "I'll also be honored if you call me Betty," she said kindly.

The festivities proceeded as guests took over the dance floor, and the evening melted into a collage of soft colors and sweet music. When the limousine arrived to take the newlyweds to the airport, Emily looked at Aaron wistfully, then went to change out of her gown for their departure.

Approaching the porch that lead to the stairway, Emily heard her in-laws' voices as they chatted behind a large evergreen. "She's such a darling," Betty was saying, "I'm afraid I scared her to death asking her to call me mom. Fortunately, I'm a realist. You can't just invite yourself to be someone's second mother. You have to earn it. And believe me, I'm going to try."

A tidal wave flooded Emily's heart. She was glad to be heading for the sanctuary of the dressing room because she was about to cry. Blessedly, only her mom was there putting the room in order.

"Honey, what's the matter?" Nancy asked, glimpsing the distress on Emily's face.

"Betty asked me to call her 'Mom,' and I just froze. For a moment, I thought she wanted to . . . well, be a substitute for you. Do I sound silly?"

"You sound sensitive. Honey, I won't feel bad if you want to call her Mom. I know your heart is big enough for two moms. You decide what's comfortable. I know you'll make the right decision."

As word spread that the newlyweds were departing, all the women gathered at the foot of the staircase. In a flurry of activity, Emily tossed her bouquet into the sea of waiting arms below, threw a

goodbye kiss in her mom's general vicinity, then bounded down the stairs with Aaron.

Hugs and kisses escorted the two along their route to the balloon-and-ribbon-festooned limo, where Aaron's parents waited. Betty pressed a box into Emily's hand. "This was my mom's," she said. "When you give it to your daughter, our family circle will continue."

"How can I thank you for everything you've done?" Emily asked, hugging her and realizing in that instant that Betty was indeed a woman she could call Mom. "See you when we get home, Mom." She looked up toward the top of the church steps, catching a glimpse of her "other" mom's smiling face as she climbed into the car.

———⊰⊱———

A MOTHER IS SHE WHO CAN TAKE THE PLACE OF ALL OTHERS
BUT WHOSE PLACE NO ONE ELSE CAN TAKE.

—*Cardinal Mermillod*

Sweet Sixteen

A week before my daughter's 16th birthday, she was moping around because she knew we were low on funds. "I'll only be 16 once," she fretted. "I want this birthday to be special."

"I'll try to make it special, Beth," I said, biting my lip when she turned away. With six mouths to feed, a roof badly in need of repair, and a stack of bills awaiting payment, how could it be as special as she hoped? My husband and I tried every way we could to stretch our budget, but we came up short.

As her birthday neared, there still didn't seem to be a solution. I sat in my recliner and nervously twisted one of my earrings. I wondered how I could give Beth the spectacular birthday she deserved.

Touching the small diamond earring brought back memories. I took it out and looked at it. The earrings had been a gift of love. My mother had had them made for me after my grandmother

had died. Now my mother was gone, too. As I wistfully replaced the earring, my thoughts turned to Beth. What could I do for her birthday?

* * *

When the day came, I could see the hope in Beth's eyes as she plopped down at the head of the table, looking eagerly at the colorful gift bag beside her plate, the red velvet cake—her favorite—gleaming with candles in the middle of the table, and the three cards near her elbow.

When Beth finished eating, she picked up the bag and said, "Can I open it?" Her big blue eyes were wide.

"Open your cards first," I said.

Beth raised an eyebrow in surprise as she read the first card out loud. "Have a happy birthday, great-granddaughter." Penned at the bottom was, "I wish I had known you, Beth. I'm sure you're a lovely girl, and I hope you enjoy your gift. Love, Great-Grandmother Irma."

A smile played tag across Beth's lips as she opened the second card. "Beth, I wish I could have seen you grow up and become a beautiful young lady. I want you to have something that was special to me. Love, Grandmother Edith."

The last card was from me. "Beth, I want you to have my gift of love. Love, Mom."

The blue eyes were full of questions as she peeled back the tissue paper. She opened the velvet-covered box to reveal the diamond stud earrings made from diamonds from her great-grandmother's watch and worn by her grandmother and her mother.

As she put the earrings into her pierced ears, a tear slipped down her cheek. Without Beth even having to say a word, I knew without a doubt I had found the perfect gift.

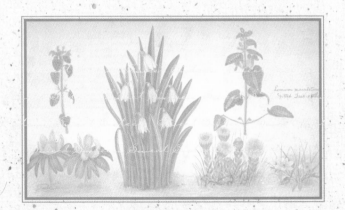

Memorial Day

I spent a recent Memorial Day afternoon with my son Michael and his wife. After we had finished grilling hamburgers and eating our fill of potato salad, we headed toward their neighborhood swimming pool.

I walked down the tree-lined street, trying to keep up with my handsome, blond-haired son, who, as usual, was three steps in front of me. He was always in a hurry, even as a small child. Suddenly, memories burst into my mind. I could see myself again as a young divorcée raising two little boys.

"Wait up, boys," I recall shouting as they raced toward the swimming pool. They slowed down long enough to throw their towels at me, then jumped in, trying to splash me in the process.

That first summer after my divorce, I found work as a secretary. Each day I came home exhausted, only to face two bored little kids, a dirty apartment, and a mountain of laundry. Every day, the boys tugged on my tired nerves, jumping around and begging to go swimming: "It's hot outside," or "Please, Mom, we're bored."

I'd take one look at the work to be done and know that I had supper to prepare, but I'd say, "Sure, let's go."

117

I spent many a late afternoon at the side of the pool mentally confronting the challenges of being a single mom: How was I going to repair the car's brakes? How would my money stretch into next month? What about the boys' birthdays? And Christmas?

It never failed, though, just when my troubles threatened to overwhelm me, I would take one look at my handsome, well-adjusted boys screaming with glee as they splashed in the pool, and I would know I was a lucky woman.

"Mom," my grown son said, breaking into my thoughts, "how does this table look?"

I started. "Oh, it's just fine." Sitting down at a green picnic table and kicking off my sandals, I basked both in the warmth of the sun and the companionship of my son and his wife. The day whizzed by, my memories all but forgotten.

A few days later, Michael called me. "Mom," he said, "I've been thinking about all those times you used to take us to the pool. You never knew this, but we spent hours trying to come up with schemes to get you there."

I laughed out loud. "Oh, I knew, Michael. I knew."

My son was serious, though. "I can't remember a single time you said you were too tired or that you had too much to do." After a pause, he added, "I see now how hard it must have been for you." He cleared his throat. "Thank you, Mom, for being there for us."

Changing Places

By the time I was six months old, I'd canoed hundreds of miles of wilderness waterway in Maine where we lived. By the age of six, I was adept at dipping my pint-sized paddle into rivers and lakes and spotting moose, bald eagles, and loons before anyone else had an inkling they were close. Soon, life-jacketed and wearing a fisherman's hat, I was sitting in the bow, or front, seat, following Mother's instructions about which side to paddle on, how to shift my weight without tipping us, and which stroke to use for changing conditions.

Mother maintained that my love of the outdoors was because she canoed and camped the whole nine months waiting for me to be born. "You must've gotten river water in your veins," she teased.

Whatever the reason, through the years we shared a growing passion for wilderness canoeing—even during my rebellious teenage years. The only time we didn't argue was on the water. I was rude, arrogant, and foolhardy—more interested in "hot-dogging" over waves than ensuring our gear arrived dry at camp. Which is why I continued paddling in the bow and my mother remained in the back, deftly steering our aluminum canoe.

Even after I went to college and, later, married, Mother and I still stole precious weekends on the water. We pulled together to reach shore in a sudden rain squall, drifting in companionable silence among cattails gone to seed. Those weekends rebuilt the bridges I had worked hard to burn as a teenager.

I guess I shouldn't have been surprised when I carried my gear to shore one morning and found Mother sitting up front in the paddler's seat.

With that changing of places, we became friends, equals, in a journey as delicate and tricky as navigating river currents.

I Love You

"My mother never told me that she loved me." That's a statement I heard recently on a tell-all TV talk show. It was offered in a lame effort to gain sympathy and to make excuses for bad behavior.

To tell the truth, I don't recall having heard my mother say the words, "I love you," either. But I didn't have to hear it said to know that it was true.

I could see it in the beauty and cheerfulness of our home, and in the soft look in Mom's eyes when she looked at me.

I could smell it in the clean clothes I put on and the freshly laundered sheets on my bed.

I could taste it in the meals Mom prepared for me each day for 20 years.

I could feel it in the warmth of her touch and the comfort and peacefulness of her presence.

Love is not just mere words; it is so much more. Something tangible, like hand-knit sweaters . . . hot chocolate waiting for you when you come in from the cold . . . brightly wrapped gifts under the Christmas tree . . . costumes for the school play . . . all the books

and writing paper you could ever ask for... homemade birthday cakes...

No, my mom didn't make a practice of telling me—in so many words—that she loved me. She didn't have to. Her actions spoke eloquently of love in a volume so loud nothing in the world could drown it out.

I was one of the lucky ones. I didn't need the words; I had the substance.

Bedtime Stories

When I was a child, we lived on a busy city street. The buses, trucks, and sparking streetcars could be heard at all hours. Our duplex had four rooms: two up and two down. None of those rooms was mine until the day my dad strapped on his work belt and created my castle in the attic. I became a princess, high above the kingdom. My castle had a small window from which I could look out and wait for my prince to rescue me from the evil witch, the mean stepmother, or the dreadful dragons.

My throne was a tiny wood-framed bed with a mattress filled with down. It was defended by a hundred stuffed animals who protected me against anyone who dared to swim the moat and invade my privacy.

Each night, the beautiful queen would glide up the spiral staircase, clutching a thick book filled with tales of my ancestors, knock gently three times on the door, and come in when I called out for her to enter. She would tiptoe across the room and settle herself next to me on the billowy cloud I called my bed.

She blew dust from the ancient tome and turned the tattered yellow pages until she reached the script we would read that evening. I ran to the great wooden door and bolted it, then slowly looked around